Some Wc

Order

LucyAnne Fletcher

Presentation by *BookLeaf Publishing*

Web: www.bookleafpub.com

E-mail: info@bookleafpub.com

ISBN: 9789358319125

First edition 2023

For Clem.

ACKNOWLEDGEMENT

Thank you Anna for proofreading and for your excellent suggestions, and Louis for allowing me to use your wonderful drawing on the cover.

The Treble Clef

In all the music I have heard
There is one figure overpassed,
Whose input, though she speaks no word,
Is tireless, wondrous, fine and vast.
That is the music of the treble clef.

Looping high above her stave
Then gliding down with hook below,
'Till every line she has enslaved
To do her bidding – there, just so!
That is the glamour of the treble clef.

Liaising with the other clefs,
Alto? Tenor? Often bass.
Accents too – she notes each stress,
And compound time, andante pace.
That is the method of the treble clef.

Keeping all the sharps in place
(Tonalities are shifty chaps)
And jostling rebels to their space –
Then once again, now with the flats.
That is the talent of the treble clef.

Her work complete, she waits, observes,
The players end their tuning notes.
Melodious fragments fill her curves
Then fade; she on their echo dotes.
That is the leisure of the treble clef.

She, more than the listening hordes
Holds every sound and tremor dear;
While others toil for poor rewards
She minds the music of our Sphere.
That is the beauty of the treble clef.

Swifts

The startling blue of midday sky was marred
By flocks of swirling swifts which glid above
And near the bench in Gables' dusty yard.
A traveller wandered close and with his glove
He gestured to the birds. "Say, is it love
That makes them fly in shapes? How do they know
Where each should put his wing, and when thereof
To soar and dive, and when instead fly slow?".
And we, the listeners, paused in thought, for we, too, did not know.

Nonsense Nose

The stars never shine
When they're set out in brine,
And the moon hums a tune
If he whistles in June.
And the leaf heaf, twig wigs, sun shun
branch kranch – But what of that?
Absolute nonsense, huffed the Nonsense Nose.

The cat is complete
When she winds her ears neat,
And the dog is a bone
If the stout hare is home.
And the fish whish, fly flights, pig dig
horse groase – But what of that?
Absolute nonsense, puffed the Nonsense Nose.

The sketch doesn't strike
When its God flaunts a bike,
And the paint spatters true
If her sigh sticks at glue.
And then pen sken, sculpt pulpts, brush wrush
mould grohwld – But what of that?
Absolute nonsense, snuffed the Nonsense Nose.

The jam eyes the juice
When the specked eggs spruce,
And the roots glimpse the shop
If the carrot dares to hop.
And the oil hoil, wine fines, herb sherb
flan glan – But what of that?
Absolute nonsense, muffed the Nonsense Nose.

The solon sparks a splash
When all's squandered in cash,
And the yarn rings like gold
If as truth wool is told.
And the law shaw, low woes, rule crool
State grate – But what of that?
Absolute nonsense, gruffed the Nonsense Nose.

The cloud feels a calm
When wrapped down in cold balm,
And the rain lands so long
With each seasonal song.
And the storm flawn, sun funs, snow plohw
wind zind – But what of that?
Absolute nonsense, kulffed the Nonsense Nose.

And he was right.

YESTERDAY

YESTERDAY you came
YESTERDAY I sighed
YESTERDAY you promised
YESTERDAY I smiled
YESTERDAY you lied
YESTERDAY I cried

YESTERDAY you left,
So my TOMORROW has DIED

Lim-Eric

There once was a young man named Eric
Who was dating another lad called Beric.
Then suddenly one day
He declared “I’m not gay!”
But the next week was caught shagging Derek.

A Meeting of Metaphors

Ah! Mr. Stevens! I'm glad I've bumped into you!
Yes, I'm glad we've crossed paths.
You see, I'd like to borrow you for a moment.
Ah, you'd like to steal me for a second?
Yes exactly, I'd like to pick your brains about this pickle we're in.
The jam we're in?
Yes exactly, as we're in the soup and all that.
Do go on.
Well as you know there's a danger of things going south.
Going downhill.
Heading in the wrong direction.
A downwards spiral.
Going to pot, exactly. And what we're really after is to cut the Gordian knot–
And knock on wood that everything will come out in the wash.
Yes exactly, but there's no denying we're currently in hot water.
Up the creek without a paddle.
Exactly, in a perfect storm, and it will be an uphill climb.
A tough nut to crack.
An uphill battle.
A tough row to hoe.
Exactly, a devil of a job. The strategy I'm currently on board with is to knuckle down–
Take the bull by the horns–
Give it everything–
Give it all we've got–
Go in all guns blazing–
Throw caution to the wind–
Exactly that, seize the day, lock stock and barrel. And, if need be, to go the whole nine yards–
Go the extra mile–
Yes, bend over backwards to move mountains. And perhaps, by the skin of our teeth, we might just rise to the occasion–
Make headway–
Make inroads–

Make a go of it–
Make the cut–
Make a comeback–
Hit the jackpot–
Hit the nail on the head–
Save the day–
Sail through–
Come up trumps–
Hit a home run–
Pass with flying colours, yes. What do you think?

Sonnet

If you were red-hot flame I'd quail and hide,
My yearning for your warmth vanquished by fear.
Or, were I bold, I would creep to your side
And singe my palms striving to hold you near.
If you were icy water I would run
For fear of drowning in your cold lagoons.
Then I'd perhaps return, having begun
To bask in lakes and trust in your monsoons.
If you were spattered earth or misty air
I'd shrink back from your sludge or eerie haze,
Craving your rocky surfaces and fair
Weather, scared by your power to amaze.
But you are you, in all your human gloire;
And I so love you 'cause of who you are.

Three Haikus

The morning dew so
Domed and perfect on the leaf
Is yesterday's rain.

The afternoon flower
So vibrant in the long grass
Is yesterday's weed.

The evening twilight
So dappled and serene was
Too cold yesterday.

Three Poems About Kittens

Curious kittens questing for kippers
Climb aboard my cataract.
I feed them, of course.

Kittens purr, kittens play,
Kittens snub and saunter away.
Kittens love cushions and sweet solitude,
But, most of all, kittens (like tigers) love food.

Kitten so tiny;
You fit in the palm of my hand!

Who-Sunnit?

A man sits slumped against the wall, head smashed.
Six suspects crowd around his billiard door,
Excitement, fear, shock, grief in all at war.
Only the butler looks on unabashed.

Rev. Green clutches his blackmail note while White
Heeds Scarlet's anguish. Mustard hates, as Plum
Dwells long on his inheritance. And, numb,
Miss Peacock recalls funds purloined last night.

But can the killer be caught with logic?
Prof. Plum was cooking. Mustard, studying.
Scarlet, reading. Peacock and Green dancing.
Ms. White quietly returns the candlestick.
Prof. Plum was cooking. Mustard, studying.
Scarlet, reading. Peacock and Green dancing.

Worry

Alone in a bubble of friends,
With thoughts so heavy they could drown an empire,
Sits Someone.

A short while ago, that Someone pondered their next
worry. Not particularly
Consciously;
It gnawed at the rinds and crusts of their thoughts, like
A tiny ribbed beetle.

Suddenly, friendships felt less congenial, happiness more transitory
and
The universe less expansive.

Until, eventually,
Someone ceased to be themself, themself thinking about
A worry, or even The Worrier.
They became The Worry itself. Not a shell of their former
Self, a mere particle.
And life feels just like a particle to them; Small. Shrivelled.
Senseless.

Limb-erick

There was a millipede with just one limb
Who vowed this occurred through her own whim.
And, pointing at a snake,
The millipede spake
"The others I hired out to him!".

It's Nearly…

In The Bleak Midwinter glistens in my thoughts, as I spot a decadent row of

T'ol' Christmas puddings. Mince pies and marzipans lie across the way, held up in triumph by a giant, jovial

Santa statue and a brightly-coloured, wood-carved

Nutcracker.

Eggnog calls invitingly from a shelf; nearby parade

Advent calendars housing chocolate, biscuits, teabags, one shaped as

Rudolph and another as nine

Ladies dancing. Oh, the

Yuletide Spirit! I close my eyes and

Carols sing through my candle-lit hearth, while

Holly winds itself along the picture-rails and mythical

Reindeer rush in and out of the paper chains, leaving

Icy trails behind them. I glance at the

Stockings, filled to bursting and waiting eagerly to be explored, when suddenly a smell of

Turkey engulfs me; the traditional Christmas roast complete with trimmings and

Mulled wine. An unexpected sound recalls my eye to an isle displaying a pyramid of

Angel figurines, but my Christmas cheer doesn't fade – Oh!

Such a pity it's only September!

A Children's Story

Bertie woke up at a quarter to twelve, and
He yawned and he stretched and he sauntered downstairs.
"Enjoy while it lasts!" an adult voice moaned,
"You cannot have lie-ins when you are full-grown!"

Bertie jumped, rolling the log to his friend, and
Then danced with delight as he caught it again.
"Enjoy while you can!" an adult voice moaned,
"You can't spend time playing when you are full-grown!"

Bertie sat waiting for dinner at six and
He drooled with delight when served sausage and steak.
"Enjoy while it's here!" an adult voice moaned,
"You don't get meals given when you are full-grown!"

Bertie gazed lovingly up from his rug at
The whole of his family sitting right there.
"Enjoy while it lasts!" an adult voice moaned,
"Your loved ones won't care so when you are full-grown!"

It's thirteen years later, and Bertie still has an
Affectionate family and food served at six.
He still wakes up late and still plays with his log,
For Bertie, in fact, is a small sausage dog.

Small Moment

Walking back home from work one day
When all was rain and gloom,
I spotted a bush nearby my way
And on it a fine white bloom.

It shone bright against its grey backdrop
Like hope budding from woe,
And lifted my spirit from the flop
It fell into long ago.

And though it was only fleetingly
I felt the flower's delight,
I know in that moment I was free –
I'd cheated earth's endless plight.

The Gull

I soar above civilisations and
Smile at the countless lines of people, love
To see them living happily
In this modern world.

In summer I fly north, admire the rain
And towering blocks that brush my wings as I
Swoop past processions of glossy
Cars and glitt'ring shops.

I laugh, as lines of people brave the cold
And sit, betowell'd, watching the waves and gulls
Dance through wet sand, armed with ice cream
And bucket and spade.

In winter I fly south, admire the din
Of motorbikes and fruit sellers as I
Glide past the dusty streets upwards
To the scorching sun.

I laugh, as lines of people sing and dance
To taarab, dressed in Kikoy and feasting,
Watching the gulls strut through the ships
And floats, pecking crumbs.

But now the rainy shores and sunny streets
Are quieter. Pinched, straggly lines of desperate
Women, men, children, queue instead
For food or a roof.

What is this ‘poverty’ that men speak of?
I am not sure. But were I human, I
Think I would not allow the lines
To grow so straggly.

A Poem in Four Parts: I – The Decision

I'm sorry, dear friend. I know I said I would phone you to discuss Friday but I've decided to have a nap instead.

A Poem in Four Parts: II – The Dream

There sits alone upon a bench
A handsome, fine young male
With smile so warm and eyes so blue
Time ne'er his looks could pale.

A voice has he divine – more pure
Than those of other men –
And all agree throughout the land
None sing so well as Glenn.

Though friends enough, he sighs one eve
For want of company;
True love he lacks (save for his voice
And fresh-brewed pot of tea!).

But as he, melancholic, se-
Renades his garden green,
His voice is by another joined,
Melodious, soft and clean.

"Approach!", cries he, and from the shrubs
Comes forth a maiden fair
All clad in robes of snow-white fur
With luscious light-brown hair.

And as the youth upon her smiles
A fire within him piques.
He falls in love just where he stands
And to her softly speaks.

"I ne'er did meet, until this night,
Enchantments such as thine,
So come, my sweet, give me your hand,
Mine with it I'll entwine.

I love you. This I'll ne'er deny
To whomesoe'er doth ask.
And from henceforth your happiness
Shall be my lifelong task.

Please tell me you'll consent, so that
Our lives might e'er be tied?
Then we shall toast to celebrate,
For I'll have found my bride!"

"I must decline" is her reply,
"I love on my own terms.
And if you truly want my hand,
You must your love affirm.

So if your passions constant prove
Then we may start anew;
In six months will it half-moon be,
I then might come for you."

In half a year returns the maid,
"I have been true!" Glenn calls,
"I wish your family to meet,
and wed you in St. Paul's!"

Entranced, into his eyes she looks,
Near spell-bound by their hue,
And in that scape of sea and sky
She sees his words are true.

"My family you then shall meet";
She wraps him in her arms.
And there they kiss, and there embrace,
Locked in each other's charms.

The lovers set about, thenceforth,
Their journey to prepare.
Glenn's brother, Benjamin, arrives,
And will not leave the pair –

"It will not do to leave you 'lone
Before you two are wed,
For passions tempt both girl and boy –
You might end up in bed!"

The three set sail next day at noon,
With all their spirits high.
The waves are kind, the wind is keen,
Their ship up North does fly.

And all the while no word does pass
Between the lovers two
Which is not kind as kind can be,
Bound in affection true.

"There's land ahoy!" Glenn's brother shouts,
"We're nearly safe and dry!"
But as he speaks the sea grows rough,
The waves break fast and high.

Both brothers from the ship are flung;
The girl echoes their cry.
Their souls are in the hand of fate –
Will they live or die?

A Poem in Four Parts: III – The Awakening

Desolation.

How can I ever recapture such a moment?
The vibrant colours, picturesque scenery,
poignant emotions?
All gone.

What is life but vivid memories?
Pictures on a canvas with broad brush-strokes,
still-life figures?
Now cartoons. Already fading.

My good friend, what am I to do?! Nothing, of course.
Desolation.

Memories can never truly be relived. And even
if they could be, what then?

Memories
can
never
truly
be
relived.

Sketches. Now faded – "Good God, get out of my head!".

And what of the two boys, and the loves, what is there fate!?

Desolation.

A Poem in Four Parts: IV – Epilogue

Engrossed, I was, with thoughts of rage and lamentation,
Anger which defied all sound persuasion
Filled with fire my cheeks, my heart, my soul – it seemed the
Dream was lost. In grief I howled and screamed.

The noise, so terrible and strange, my own heart chilled, and
Filled with ice and dread I lay, eyes wide with
Yearning strong for slumber. Also with remorse. Oh
Would I had my speech made far less coarse!

And whilst, dear friend, I sprawled in throes of such unrest, a
Memory keen and potent on me pressed – no
Rest can come, the Book declares, unto the sinner;
So, with sufferance great, went I to dinner.

The Greek Temple

Long-columned, stretching to misty nothings,
Stand the remnants of an old Greek chapel.
Former sovereign of the realm, its stone clings,
Stoic, to glory, shunning the grapple
With modern life, unaware its craggy
Structures now survive immortalised on
Sterile canvas. Crumbling steps and claggy
Rubble are its subjects; vot'ries long gone.
New devotees in galleries admire
Brushwork; yet the iron-willed capitals bear
Proudly still their absent load, and aspire
To an artistry beyond human care.

Milton Keynes UK
Ingram Content Group UK Ltd.
UKHW020649040424
440620UK00014B/565